HOLDING ON

Patricia Holman

**The true story of a mother's loss of her
only child and her husband**

UNICORN PRESS

First published 1997 by Unicorn Press
21 Afghan Road
London SW11 2QD

A CIP catalogue record for this book is available
from the British Library

ISBN 0 906290 16 3

Typeset by Galleon Typesetting, Ipswich
Printed in Great Britain by
Redwood Books, Trowbridge, Wiltshire

Dedication and Acknowledgements

I dedicate this book to the past and present neighbours of Kaywood, also to Trevor's friends. Without their continued support I would have been unable to pick up the threads of life.

My love and gratitude to my parents, my sister Jean and family; and to Terry and Carole for their practical and emotional support.

I would also like to thank the Salvation Army and the Compassionate Friends for the assistance and support they have given me.

My thanks to my dear friend Jenny, who typed the text and patiently supported me through all the pain and emotional distress I suffered while reliving the tragedy for this book.

I also thank Andrew Crofts for his advice and help in the structuring of my story.

To Michael Day, my thanks for his original idea for the front cover and Stuart Squires of Simon Girling & Associates for the finished artwork. Photographs by kind permission of Dave Cox and Jean Needs.

Pat with her parents and husband, Gerry, in happier times

Contents

Foreword

This is the story of my own personal tragedy. I am writing it in the hope that it will help and comfort others.

I was busy and happy before disaster struck and shattered my whole existence. It started when my precious only child went missing with no explanation. When he was found dead in mysterious circumstances I not only had to cope with bereavement but did not know how or why he had died. Then my dear husband and several cherished friends became ill and died and I had to search even further within myself for the strength to hold on.

Never did I foresee such devastation, nor that my life would suddenly seem so useless. What was the point in carrying on?

During my darkest hours there emerged certain pillars of strength and they have helped me to live with the knowledge that I shall never see my son or my husband again in this life.

If the following story helps even one person in any one of these situations then it will have been worth the telling.

CHAPTER 1

The Beginning

It was Saturday, two weeks before Christmas, 1988 and I was in bed with flu. My temperature was high and I kept drifting in and out of sleep, more or less oblivious to what was going on around me. What happened on that fateful day was to change the rest of my life.

Gerald, my husband, or Gerry as he was known, had spent a disturbed night listening to me coughing and wheezing but reluctantly dragged himself out of bed at 7 a.m., aware that there was Christmas shopping to be done. He made me a light breakfast but didn't disturb Trevor, our only son, the love and joy of my life, who was still sleeping.

Trevor had been out to the pub the night before with his pals and didn't have to work on Saturdays. He was still asleep at around 9 a.m. when Gerry left the house and drove into Windsor. While my husband was out, Trevor got up and answered the door to Hilda, a friend of mine who had called to see if I was feeling any better.

'He wasn't his usual friendly self,' she told me later, 'he didn't seem to want to ask me in. I thought it must be because he was still in his dressing gown, so I just left the flowers and said I hoped you would be up and about soon.'

I do remember Trevor calling out, 'Mum, it's Hilda,' but all I could reply was 'Oh, is it? I'm in bed,' in a rather weak voice.

'I was surprised by his vagueness,' Hilda said. 'On the way to my car I hesitated and thought about going back and knocking again, but changed my mind. I got in the car and drove off. All through that day I found myself thinking how withdrawn Trevor had seemed.'

By the time Gerry arrived back at midday, Trevor had put Hilda's flowers in water, vacuumed downstairs and was sitting, watching Grandstand. Having greeted his son, Gerry came upstairs to see if I was okay, placing the gifts he had bought on the dressing table.

'I'll make you a hot lemon drink,' he said, 'then I must get off to Slough to buy another couple of presents.' As he hurried downstairs I heard him call out to Trevor, 'the shops are very busy and parking is difficult. If you want a lift to Slough I'm leaving in five minutes.'

Through my haze of illness I was aware of Trevor getting ready in his bedroom. He was planning to buy a pair of steps for his dad's Christmas present and I knew he needed to get some other things, including some face lotion for me. I had given him the name of the one I liked, which he wrote on a small notepad. When he left the house he took the sheet of paper with him, leaving the pad with the impression on in his room. He looked in on me before going downstairs again and asked for some suggestions for presents. I felt too sleepy to be co-operative. He left me in peace and that was the last time I was to see Trevor.

At about 12.15 p.m. my husband and son drove off together. When they reached Slough the multi-storey car park was full so Gerry parked in the local Lascelles Park and they walked towards the High Street, passing the recently opened Co-op store.

'What with the new Tesco coming,' Trevor commented, 'and the existing supermarket in the High Street, one of them is bound to go under.'

The DIY shop where they were going to buy the steps was at the beginning of the High Street. They each bought a pair because Gerry wanted some for outside renovation. He was about to take early retirement at the age of 59 and was looking forward to all the little jobs that needed doing around the house, as well as spending more time on hobbies like his art. He still intended to work a couple of days a week at the Trust Company of a major bank which had been his employer for nearly thirty years, but all the pressure which had been giving him so much stress in recent years was going to be taken away at last.

The shopkeeper agreed to hold on to their purchases for later collection. They walked on down the street, chatting quite normally until they reached one of the larger stores that Gerry wanted to go into. They paused for a moment and said goodbye cheerfully to each other. Trevor went off up the High Street to buy a snack lunch and do the rest of his shopping. That was the last time my husband ever saw him.

Finishing his shopping, Gerry collected the car and drove round to pick up the steps. He then came home to see if there was anything extra I needed before setting off again for Windsor. I was fast asleep when he finally got back between 3 and 3.30 p.m. and so he decided to delay making me a cup of tea and left me sleeping.

At around 5.15 p.m. I began frantically screaming for Gerry. He rushed upstairs and found me sitting bolt upright in bed with beads of sweat running down my face. I grabbed hold of him desperately. 'I've had a premonition,' I gasped, 'that something awful has happened to Trevor.'

Gerry took a tissue and gently wiped the perspiration from my face. 'You've got a temperature,' he said soothingly, 'you're hallucinating.'

Half an hour later I was becoming very agitated and concerned that Trevor had not returned home. 'He's twenty-two years old,' Gerry reasoned calmly, 'there's nothing unusual in him spending some time in a high street.'

Just after 6 p.m. Stuart, a friend of Trevor's, and his girlfriend, Ruth, called at our house on their way home from a football match, expecting to find Trevor. The previous evening, Stuart arranged with him that he would call so they could discuss their Saturday plans. He left a message for Trevor to meet them at Ruth's house and asked if he could ring to confirm that it was on for Saturday night. Although Gerry thought I was making a fuss, he realised it was unlike me to show unnecessary concern and thought it best to telephone Trevor's friends. None of them had seen Trevor, but nobody seemed to think it likely there was a problem.

Still feeling terrible, I could no longer bear to stay in bed. My insides felt tight with anxiety as I strained to see through the windows into the darkness outside, watching the main road and the buses going past, holding my breath each time, waiting for one of the hurrying figures to turn the corner. But they just kept passing by the end of the road. I had never been so certain that something dreadful had happened. 'If you keep walking about with that high temperature,' Gerry fussed, 'standing close to windows, you could be very ill.'

I kept pestering him to call the police, so by 9 p.m. he had finally agreed that something unusual must have happened and telephoned our local police station in Langley. I waited, trembling with fear, as Gerry explained the situation. My hands moved up to my face as if to push away the distant voice of the policeman.

'Trevor is an adult,' the voice reasoned with us, 'he can come and go as he wishes.'

'It's out of character,' Gerry argued, becoming rather agitated, 'Trevor would let us know if he was unable to get home.' Trevor had always been a sensitive and understanding boy. He drove a hard bargain but was so honest that even if he took a postage stamp from my purse he always replaced it with the correct amount of money. He wouldn't deliberately cause us to worry like this, we were both sure of that.

There was nothing the police could do at that stage, we just had to wait. Gerry became more and more anxious as the minutes ticked by and I felt sick with worry. Late that night we could stand it no longer and Gerry rang the police again with me clinging to his arm.

'Do you know of Trevor's plans for Sunday?' the officer asked.

'All we know,' Gerry replied, 'is that he has made arrangements to meet his girlfriend, Beth. She's a trainee nurse. They were to meet at the local swimming pool at 3 p.m.'

'At the moment, sir,' the officer replied 'I suggest you keep in touch with us and let us know of any fresh information.'

CHAPTER 2

The First Long Day

We both slept fitfully, waking every couple of hours. The main lights in the house had been left on all night. At around 6 a.m. Gerry got up and dressed. The lights were still on so we knew Trevor had not come home without us hearing. I lay in bed staring out of the window as dawn broke. Our neighbours' trees loomed up into the winter sky, dwarfing the houses. My stomach was churning with anxiety. During the night I had glanced into Trevor's room. Seeing the unslept-in bed, covered with the dark brown candlewick bedspread, had filled me with fear.

As well as feeling terribly washed out from the flu, my back was hurting badly and getting dressed was a struggle. I must have stretched or torn some muscle or ligament by getting up too soon the day before.

When it was fully light Gerry telephoned the police again and they promised to come round to the house in an hour. Before they arrived the doorbell rang and my heart missed a beat. I dropped the night clothes I had in my hand and ran down the stairs. Gerry had got to the front door before me. On the doorstep were two of my teenage ballet students, calling with Christmas gifts. Having asked them into the hall Gerry then disappeared to the kitchen.

'Are you ill, Mrs Holman?' one of the girls asked when they saw me, 'you look very pale.'

'Just recovering from a slight bout of flu,' I answered hesitantly, aware that one of them was the daughter of the local newspaper editor, and wondering if I should ask her father to telephone me. I chose to say nothing yet, unable to decide whether to suppress the story, knowing Trevor could not abide any fuss, or to give it as much publicity as possible. Trevor would hate to have his private life exposed in this way, but at the same time the idea of us all getting in such a state might tickle his sense of humour.

Once the girls had gone I explained my dilemma to Gerry, who, being rather inclined to be a private man, replied cautiously, 'my feelings are that we should wait and see what the police advise.'

Two policemen arrived just after 10 a.m. Feeling very disturbed by their presence in our home, and light-headed from the flu, I found if difficult to concentrate on their questions. During the interview they asked for a recent photograph of Trevor.

'We don't have one that recent,' I explained, 'Our son was always the one behind the camera, you see. He was such a good organiser, planning the routes when he and his friends went on holidays, also, Trevor was blessed with a good memory . . .' I could see that one of them was looking at me as if to say, 'I bet this young man has gone off on some trip that took his fancy.'

They suggested that they should interview all his close friends and asked us to get them over to the house that afternoon. Once they had gone, Gerry telephoned five of Trevor's friends and Beth, his girlfriend, explaining what had happened and making arrangements for them to come round at 3 p.m. The only one who couldn't make it was Paul, because he was working.

We all gathered in the lounge, sitting in a large circle. I kept moving from chair to floor, dragging a cushion behind me, trying to ease my back. Gerry looked drawn and everyone was mystified as to what could have happened. Please God, I thought, let me wake up soon and find this was just a dreadful nightmare. Even before coming over, Trevor's friends had been combing the area looking for him.

A policeman spoke to each of them in turn, but no one could throw any light on the matter. One boy remembered that on the previous Friday evening at the local pub, Trevor seemed to have a far-away look in his eyes, sort of staring into space.

'A few days ago,' I said, 'he did receive a blow to the

head. It happened at work when a large tin box fell off a shelf, causing momentary semi-consciousness. Unfortunately, he did not receive hospital treatment. Perhaps he could be suffering from a delayed memory loss.' Trevor worked for the RAC, organising car rallies, and they had been preparing for a visit from their President, Prince Michael of Kent. Trevor had been due, with a colleague, to show the Prince round and had been doing some tidying up when the box fell. Instead of sending him to hospital for a check-up they put him in a taxi and, on arriving home, I found him on the settee with a cold flannel clutched to his head.

The boys suggested that he might have gone to Leicester or Nottingham. Apparently they had met a couple of lads from the area whilst on holiday in Majorca. Sadly, none of them could remember their addresses. They all chuckled and admitted if anyone had kept the information in his head it would have been Trevor. One of them gave the detective sergeant a photograph of him. It was a good likeness. The police told us they would pass all the information on to the main police stations throughout the country. After they had gone, Trevor's friends went back to searching the area, returning to the house later that evening, looking very downcast, with nothing to report.

'Yesterday,' I told them, 'when coming round from that premonition, I felt that something had happened to Trevor. I remember thinking that he was in some way associated with a turret-like building, like the one on the edge of Lascelles Park. Please go and look there once more.' They did as I asked and searched thoroughly, but found nothing.

CHAPTER 3

Christmas and the New Year

By Monday the neighbours were beginning to wonder what was going on in our house, having seen the police and Trevor's friends coming and going at all hours. Eva was a retired nursing sister who lived in a large house opposite ours and Jean lived next door to her. When they called round we explained what had happened. They were alarmed by the way I looked. On hearing that we had hardly eaten since Saturday, they returned later with Complan and Lucozade and I was able to keep a little of it down. I didn't really feel like eating anything but desperately wanted to get my strength back in order to go out searching for Trevor with the others.

Gerry was concentrating on organising things, trying to work out the best way forward. He telephoned his office and told a colleague that he couldn't come in because I was too ill with the flu to be left alone. He decided to say nothing about Trevor at that stage. He went down into Slough and retraced his route in the High Street, showing Trevor's photograph to staff in the shops. In Boots the chemist, where Trevor would have gone to buy my face lotion, a young assistant thought she had served him. 'He was undecided about what to buy,' she told Gerry, 'and went away without a purchase.'

The police paid us another visit. They wanted to search the loft, garden shed, garage and everywhere else. It was as if we were under suspicion as they pulled everything out and examined it. Even an old rolled up carpet was hauled out of the roof and spread flat to check we hadn't hidden his body in there. By the time they left we both felt completely shattered as if our whole life had been invaded.

There were still no clues as to what could have happened. We made enquiries at Slough coach and train stations because, in the past, he had often picked up a coach for London from the top of our close to go to a football match or some other sporting event at the other end of the country. Gerry telephoned Victoria Coach Station to see if they had any record of Trevor making a booking or passing through, but there was no trace.

Beth's parents, who we had never met, called to introduce themselves and offer their support. They asked if we would like them to get in touch with John, our priest, saying they knew him quite well as Beth's father was also in the church, but we decided not to go to him just yet. They told us what a polite and happy person Trevor had seemed to them. Like us, they were at a loss to know where he could be.

We were still torn between holding back the news that Trevor was missing and publicizing his disappearance. Part of me kept thinking, if he opens the front door and sees a policeman, then hears all about the exposure of his private life he'll never forgive us; but the other part wanted to spread the word around as far as possible.

That evening the news was full of the Clapham rail disaster. One of Gerry's brothers telephoned from Cheshire to see if any of us had been on the train. We reassured him that we were not travelling at the time of the accident and didn't mention our personal problems, not wanting to worry the family unnecessarily. There was, of course, always the possibility that Trevor could have been on the train.

The days and nights seemed to roll together into an extended nightmare. As the news leaked out, many people came to make enquiries and Gerry was brewing endless cups of tea for everyone who called. Sympathy cards, letters and flowers arrived daily and we frequently had a police car parked outside the house. Trevor's friends were very supportive and visited us regularly. For me it all seemed unreal, as if I was sleepwalking through life.

Jean, my sister, was expecting us for Christmas with Mum and Dad. We decided, at the end of the week, that she should be told what was happening. She was very shocked by the news and rang us regularly for updates. 'I can't concentrate at work,' she told us, 'I keep bursting into tears but all my office colleagues are very understanding.' Her main worry was how she could keep it from Mum and Dad. We were all nervous about how such worrying news might affect their health.

Gerry was retiring from work on 23 December. A party had been arranged, not only for colleagues at his Ealing branch, but also for people from London head office. It was a formal event, involving caterers and Gerry decided not to cancel. We tried to remain positive, to believe that Trevor would return before then, that he would be home for Christmas and that we must be ready for him. The thought of attending a celebration with him still missing didn't bear thinking about.

Gerry had joined the Trust Company of a major bank in 1961, becoming a Trust Officer in 1974. Some of his work involved the drawing up of wills and advising people on how to invest their money. He had moved several times in his career, finally ending up in Ealing at the end of the 1970s.

In the end, the party had to go ahead without us and we had to explain our problem. Right up till the last minute we hoped that Trevor would be back in time. Terry, a friend and colleague of Gerry's, agreed to accept a gift token on his behalf and said a few words of thanks to the staff. Carole, his wife, told me that it was some time before Terry could bring himself to talk about the party, it had proved to be such an enormous strain. Terry had known Trevor ever since he was young, when we all lived in Essex and he often travelled back from work with Gerry on Friday evenings and had dinner with us. The three of them used to go off and support Southend United afterwards.

We tried to keep the façade of our normal life going as much as possible, sending out our Christmas cards with no reference to Trevor's disappearance. We didn't feel able to handle all the extra sympathy calls and visitors there were bound to be if everyone knew. Part of us was trying to pretend none of it was happening, trying to lose our unhappiness in familiar routines whenever possible.

We contacted Trevor's bank and building society and asked them to let us know if any money was taken out of his account. They very kindly rang us at the end of every working day to say that, yet again, no withdrawals had been made.

We had found two tickets in Trevor's bedroom for a football match at Queens Park Rangers on 17 December in London – he was a QPR supporter. Apparently he and Stuart had arranged to go. Gerry and Stuart decided to go together, scanning the crowds inside and outside the ground for any sign of Trevor. The management agreed to broadcast an announcement over the loudspeaker during the game – 'if Trevor Holman is with us today, would he please contact his parents after the match'.

Gerry left the stadium before the end of play to get a good viewing position from which to observe the crowds as they came out. As the hordes of fans pushed and jostled their way past, their faces often obscured in QPR hats and scarves, Gerry and Stuart peered desperately for a glimpse of Trevor's familiar features. They came home that evening exhausted and disappointed.

The police had been very helpful in guarding our privacy but, as the days rolled on, they advised us that we should now give Trevor's disappearance as much publicity as possible. We started by informing John, our priest, and asked him to let our close friends at the church know what was happening. He called round the next day to say that he had done that and had also been in touch with Families Anonymous and the Salvation Army. He gave us the relevant information and suggested we get in contact with both organisations.

As one of the local newspaper editors knew of me through his daughter attending my ballet classes, I telephoned him at his home to explain our problem. He reassured me that the newspaper would handle the story in a sensitive manner. Gerry contacted the *Daily Mirror*, who were interested in running a story, and other press offices which covered local news.

Gerry did most of the telephoning. I still felt so ill from a mixture of flu, back pain and anxiety that I just lay on the settee in a complete daze most of the time. He kept a small notebook which contained the names of the different policemen who had visited us and the times they came on and off duty. He listed all Trevor's friends and family members with their home and work telephone numbers, so that we could contact anyone at any time in an emergency. LBC agreed to broadcast an announcement over the radio.

News travelled fast once we had made it official, resulting in an incessant stream of telephone calls and visits. No one believed that the confident, extrovert, likeable young man they had known could disappear without a trace. Because of my persistent flu symptoms everyone advised me to stay at home and so I answered most of the calls. Every time the telephone rang my heart missed a beat and I would pick up the receiver saying, 'Is that you, Trevor?' my spirits plummeting the moment I heard another voice. Everyone we knew told us they were continually on the look-out for Trevor, often mistaking strangers for him. When Jean, my neighbour, saw a young man in a telephone box who seemed similar to him, she waited anxiously until she had a clearer view before moving on.

On Christmas Eve, neighbours and friends called with gifts of food and flowers. Jean and Geoff invited us to their house opposite for Christmas dinner. They suggested that we sat near the window, so that we could keep an eye on our front door in case Trevor returned. It was a kind thought but we said we would rather stay at home, close to the telephone. As Christmas Eve came to an end Gerry said: 'I think we have seen the last of the callers, I'll lock up.' But there was one last ring on the bell. It was Trevor's closest friend, Kevin, standing in the dim light, holding a Christmas plant. I shall always remember how sad he looked, summing up the absolute desolation we all felt.

Kevin and Trevor had an extraordinary bond, even though they frequently rowed and argued. They were like brothers, neither ever bearing any grudges. Trevor had said to me only a few weeks before, 'you know Mum, if I committed a crime, Kevin would always shield me.'

'Most people,' I replied, 'go all through their lives and never find a friend like that.'

Christmas Day seemed unreal. In a daze I prepared a light lunch, then we stared with vacant eyes at the television. The hours dragged past as I lay on the settee in the lounge, watching the darkness gradually submerging the room. We were both longing for night to come so that we could take the sleeping tablets the doctor had prescribed and block out everything.

Christmas was not easy for my sister, Jean, either. We had managed to keep the news from Mum and Dad, but they were very puzzled by the way we were behaving. 'I can't understand,' Mum told Jean, 'why Pat, Gerry and Trevor haven't come to spend Christmas with us as usual.' Jean told her that we were tired after the retirement party and that Trevor was visiting his friend Paul in Norwich. 'They're going to watch Norwich play football on Boxing Day,' she lied. Watching the game on television, Mum and Dad kept saying they could see the boys in the stands. Later that evening they wanted Trevor's music played, saying that they missed him organising all the entertainment. Jean walked the dog many times, just to get out of the house and collect her thoughts.

Trevor and his two close friends, Kevin and Paul

The Lockerbie disaster filled the news at that time and Trevor's disappearance never made it into the *Daily Mirror* though it was front page news in our local press and the Slough newspapers continued to give us weekly coverage.

Involving the newspapers had its downside as well. Beth's father was a local vicar and that year he was chaplain to the Mayor of Slough. An insensitive journalist, acting on false information, tried to create a scandal. He went snooping around their garden, peering in at the windows until the vicar challenged him.

'Is it true,' the journalist asked, 'that your daughter's boyfriend, the one who's missing, was having an affair with your wife?' One quick telephone call to the newspaper put a stop to that story.

During that period many of our friends and family received mysterious telephone calls. The caller never spoke, but everyone had a feeling of Trevor's presence. My sister received two of these calls over the holiday. 'I just felt somehow it was Trevor trying to contact us,' she said.

My next problem was that it would soon be time to start the new term of my ballet schools. When we moved to Slough at the beginning of the 1980s, the Vicar of St Francis, a small church close to our home, called to make us welcome. He told me that the church was also used as a community hall and suggested it could be used for ballet classes. At the time I had already decided to teach in the village of Datchet, just outside

Windsor. But, because the church was so close and the congregation so friendly, we joined as worshippers and I ended up running classes in the two locations. Both businesses were a success and had led to me, like Gerry, working at full stretch as Trevor grew up.

It was a great relief when two of my students' mothers offered to deliver letters to other parents advising of a delay in starting the dancing term. I had not ventured outside the house since Trevor's disappearance but, on New Year's Eve, I realised that I needed to buy a card for Gerry's birthday on 1 January. My friend, Carole, offered to accompany me to the shops. It was a strange experience. In the busy street everyone was dashing around, doing their shopping, unaware of what was happening to me. I wanted to shout, 'Stop! Don't you know, my son is missing?'

No words could express what I wanted to say on the birthday card. The only words my husband wanted to hear were from Trevor, saying, 'Happy Birthday, Dad'. I knew, deep in my heart, that Trevor would never have forgotten his father's birthday. I was becoming more and more certain that something terrible had happened. Kevin told me that he too was now beginning to have some doubts.

Just before the New Year we decided we should break the news to Mum and Dad in case they heard it through the media. Jean's husband, Harry, told Dad. He remained very calm and then told Mum about it in his own way. To begin with she couldn't accept what she was hearing. 'I don't believe it,' was all she kept saying. We were all very worried about what it would do to her high blood pressure.

Following New Year, I made innumerable visits to my doctor and physiotherapist about my back problem, thinking, I've got to get better so that I can look for Trevor. I would sit in the car in agonizing pain as Gerry drove me around. The neighbours volunteered to man the telephone whenever we went out. The doctor told me that stress was the reason it wasn't mending.

Gerry continued the publicity campaign, making contact with the Nottingham Evening Post, telling them that Trevor and his friends had, in the past, enjoyed a weekend break in the area. We wanted to catch the eye of the lads they had met whilst on holiday in Majorca. The paper placed the story on the front page and that weekend Stuart and his girlfriend, Ruth, went to a football match in the area, showing a picture of Trevor around the ground and at a pub they had all visited the previous trip. They got no response and neither did we.

On 20 January it was my mother's eightieth birthday, but all the family celebrations were cancelled. We decided to visit them in West Sussex with Jean and Harry, staying at a small hotel near their home so as not to put them to any trouble. We told the police exactly what our movements would be and the neighbours were going to keep an eye on the house for us. It was the first time we had left the telephone unattended since Trevor's disappearance and the thought of it made me feel very uneasy. I knew, however, that it was only for the weekend and that it was important that we do something for Mum and Dad.

We took them out for a meal on the Saturday night but I was very nervy and hardly ate anything. I left the table several times to find somewhere quiet where I could take a few deep breaths and ward off the minor panic attacks which gripped me. We took Mum and Dad home after the meal and wearily returned to our beds in the hotel.

Early on the Sunday morning the manager of the hotel received a telephone call from the Berkshire police asking to speak to us. They had already rung my parents, even though we had left them the hotel number. Gerry took the call. They said they had removed a young man, who resembled Trevor, from the Thames and asked if someone could make a formal identification. Gerry telephoned our friend and neighbour, Eva, knowing that as a retired nursing sister she would be able to cope with a task like this better than most, and asked her if she would do it. She agreed and went with her eldest son. 'I'll telephone you from the hospital mortuary,' she promised.

The next half an hour was like waiting for a guillotine blade to fall. The hotel manager, sensing the gravity of the situation, found me a chair and a glass of brandy, but

I couldn't sit still and frequently found myself walking out into the garden, standing on the cold concrete patio, taking deep breaths to try to keep myself together. Gerry and Harry paced up and down by the telephone, their foreheads glistening with sweat while Jean went to get a glass of water and busied herself at the public payphone, searching for the local doctor's telephone number in case the worst happened.

Finally the call came. 'The young man has a likeness to Trevor,' Eva told us, 'but I'm sure it's not him.'

The police then asked us to return to Berkshire to make a positive identification. Relieved by Eva's call, Jean and I realised that my parents would be very shocked to have received the initial call and Jean telephoned their doctor, asking him to visit them as soon as possible. Leaving the men to settle the hotel bill and collect the car, we made our way up the unmade, muddy road to Mum and Dad's flat on foot. Jean was wearing high heels and kept missing her footing. As we stumbled along, nervous and breathless, the winding road seemed to go on forever. We arrived at their home almost at the same time as the doctor, finding Mum and Dad reasonably okay.

Mum said she had never believed it was Trevor in the mortuary. She had this idea that he had taken himself off somewhere like America and would return home one day, laden with duty free gifts for us all. Dad was not so optimistic. As soon as Gerry and Harry arrived with the car we said our goodbyes to the family and left for Berkshire.

'The police said that the young man was wearing a green jacket when he was lifted from the Thames,' Gerry remembered as we drove along. As soon as we arrived home we rushed to the downstairs hall cupboard to check that Trevor's green anorak was hanging on its hook. We both stood staring at it in absolute relief.

Windsor mortuary was a terrifying experience. We had to wait for over an hour at Langley police station for an escort because there had been a major traffic accident and all the senior officers were busy. They suggested that Gerry should make the identification. As I watched him walking towards the mortuary from the police car I felt sick with anguish.

After spending some time looking at the young man, Gerry told them that he was not sure if it was Trevor and thought I should make the identification. 'Do you think we should put your wife through this ordeal?' the Inspector asked.

'I don't know,' said Gerry who was very distressed. 'I don't know. I just don't know whether it is Trevor.' They came out and asked me to make an identification.

Trembling with fear I entered the mortuary. Closing my eyes, I took a deep breath before looking at the face of the young man who seemed to be peacefully asleep. He did resemble Trevor. I wanted to walk round and round him, searching for clues.

'His toe nails look as though they need attention,' I said to the attendant, 'they are very similar to my son's.'

'Most young men I see have toe nails like that,' he told me.

The police decided I had seen enough and persuaded me to leave, suggesting that a positive identification be made from finger prints in Trevor's bedroom and his dental records. The following day they got the prints and visited our dentist. Within a few hours we knew that the young man taken from the Thames was not Trevor.

'I never want to see Windsor again,' Gerry said when the whole affair was over.

Trevor and his friends had had several weekend breaks in Brighton and Hove, so Gerry made contact with the editor of the *Brighton Evening Argus* who agreed to publish a picture and details. A lady home-help then wrote to us, via the newspaper, saying that she was sure she had seen Trevor in Eaton Road, Hove. Our hopes soared and we immediately made arrangements to visit the area. Before leaving my GP administered a cortisone injection in my lower back as it was still troublesome. We set off, armed with pain-killing tablets, sandwiches and a flask of coffee.

Checking with the Hove police was our first priority. Waiting while an officer telephoned round the hospitals and DHSS, I was aware of the watery, winter sun shining into the sparsely furnished station, making the atmosphere hot and stuffy. Every now and again, as my weight shifted from foot to foot, I would inhale the stale, musty air. They found no trace of Trevor but recommended a small hotel that was close to the shops and police station.

The drab room we were given contained a small basin with a dripping tap. Gerry mentioned it to the manager, who moved us to yet another dowdy room. It was adequate, a place frequented by travelling salesmen and policemen on short stays in the area. Neither of us was interested in luxury, just wanting somewhere convenient to sleep. Walking along the corridor, I was aware of the stagnant smell of cigarette smoke which clung to the fabric of the landing and hallway. Throughout the first afternoon we walked the length of Hove, visiting sports centres, cafés, newsagents and betting shops. I was struck by how strange it felt to see other people enjoying themselves, oblivious to our pain. The familiar life had vanished and we had been left existing in some kind of hellish vacuum. Both of us were bewildered and lost, wondering all the time what to do next, clutching at every straw, each grateful for any idea the other might come up with.

Towards the end of the afternoon we decided to visit a holiday camp outside Brighton at Saltdean. Trevor had had a liking for camp holidays; perhaps he might be working there as casual labour. The sea looked rough and frothy from the cliff top. Being January it was very quiet and I stayed in the car while Gerry made enquiries at the camp hotel. No one had any knowledge of Trevor having worked there but we decided all the same to have a look around ourselves. With a great deal of back pain I climbed out of the car. A strong bitterly cold, south wind was blowing round the car park and outside buildings. Gerry stopped one or two people, showing Trevor's photographs, but nobody had seen him. It was a relief to get into the shelter of the foyer of the camp hotel, away from the biting wind. Having looked in the games room, ballroom and swimming pool area, we decided to concentrate on Hove where the positive sighting had been.

The next day we called on launderettes and dry cleaners and a motherly, rosy-cheeked woman said she thought Trevor had been in on the Monday of that week, returning on the Wednesday to collect his clothes. At last we were getting somewhere, we thought. He must be somewhere close, it could only be a matter of time before someone found him, but how much time? We left a photograph and several telephone numbers with the woman, asking her to make contact should he reappear. That evening Gerry took me to an up-market restaurant for a meal, concerned that I wasn't eating enough. I chose something light from the extensive menu but could do no more than pick at it.

'If you don't eat,' Gerry said anxiously, 'you won't keep up your strength.'

On the Friday we went to numerous pubs. At the Sussex Cricketer, whilst I was waiting for Gerry to come back from showing the landlord Trevor's picture, I saw through the window a young man who resembled Trevor. He was on the other side of the street, walking towards the shops. I rushed out of the pub, mingling with the crowd, trying to catch him up, but soon lost sight of him. He seemed to just vanish amongst the shoppers. A few minutes later Gerry caught me up and we lingered for a couple of hours on street corners. Standing outside an open-plan greengrocers, I was jostled by the many shoppers, my tired eyes searching the crowd for the young man I had lost. Later that afternoon, having left telephone numbers and photographs with many people, we returned to Slough. Gerry had the feeling that someone else would soon recognise him and more than likely telephone our home.

Soon after our return home, Kevin and Stuart called round. The four of us were discussing our experiences in Hove when the telephone rang. No one spoke on the other end. 'My 'phone rang just before I left home to take my driving test the other day,' Stuart told us after we had hung up, 'I picked it up and it was silent. I said, "Is that you Trev?" And after a few seconds the line went dead. Perhaps he was thinking about me and wanted to wish me luck. As I passed the test it must have done the trick. I wish he was here so that I could tell him.'

Towards the end of January, Gerry and I visited a psychiatrist to try to find out why someone, seemingly leading a happy, normal life, should suddenly disappear. The visit was fruitless. I kept thinking, where do we go from here?

Kevin and his girlfriend, Helen, decided to go down to Hove and call on many of the places we had visited. Family and friends alike thought keeping Trevor's description fresh in the public's memory was important. On their return, everyone tried to think of other places in the area that might bring more positive results. It was all we had to work on.

CHAPTER 4

Devastation

On 1 February, 1989 we received another silent telephone call. Both Gerry and I spoke into the receiver as if Trevor was there, urging him to talk to us, but there was no answer. After a few minutes the telephone made a bell like sound and then the line went dead. Our friends and neighbours continued to have similar experiences. Gerry paid a second visit to QPR, staying outside the ground, watching the crowd. He looked so tired on his return home.

We booked another trip to Hove for 14 February, staying at the same hotel. My back pain was still bad and the doctor told me that stress was now the prime factor in making it slow to improve. The only footwear I could tolerate were sandals and the weather was bitterly cold.

Neither the Hove police nor the woman in the washeteria had any news for us. We trudged along the main street to Brighton, stopping at McDonalds and Wimpy to show Trevor's picture. A young man in

Wimpys said that he had served Trevor the day before and later had seen him outside a telephone box in Churchill Square. His friend confirmed this. They said he was wearing a leather jacket, which was unfamiliar to us. We left the photograph and our telephone numbers with the young man and spent the rest of the day near to the telephone box he had pointed out in Churchill Square, a couple of blocks off the Brighton seafront. People got on and off buses, others looked suspicious as they loitered in the shadows. We frequently approached passers-by and showed them Trevor's photograph. As the day was coming to an end, workers hurried from their offices and shops, many making for the square to catch transport home. Gerry repeatedly approached drivers of the rush hour buses, holding Trevor's picture high, leaning into their warm cabs as they racked their memories. Conductors held up their departures as they pondered over Trevor's face and I mingled with the waiting queues, desperately asking if anyone had seen someone resembling our missing son. Nothing.

It was dark on the way back to our hotel room. I was desperate for some semblance of normality and tried to find it on the television, pushing the remote control buttons from station to station as if trying to get back to my previous life. Gerry blocked a gaping, drafty hole in the skirting board with a towel and we fell asleep, knowing that there were more roads, more hotels and the unknown underworld to comb the following day.

Next came visits to the many large hotels on the Brighton seafront with their palatial foyers full of chatter and laughter. Then on to job agencies, leaving Trevor's name and our telephone number. The early afternoon found us drifting in and out of nightclubs. I felt very uncomfortable standing in this alien world with bouncers hovering in the background. Although my back was constantly painful, I felt we had to climb those many staircases and descend all those rusty iron steps that led to seedy rooms, in case Trevor was there. In my heart I felt it was hopeless, it just wasn't Trevor's scene, but we had to keep searching.

That afternoon we returned home in case there had been any further developments in Slough. Once more Kevin and Helen came back to Hove and Brighton to repeat the exercise. Like us, they found those visits very stressful. They would sit in their car for long periods, scrutinising young people. 'It's him!' one would say as a young man resembling Trevor walked towards them. Then they would be disappointed once more. The feeling was, we mustn't let up. During February we received a visit from a couple whose son had been reported missing in the Surrey area. Later, they sent us the literature on how to cope when someone goes missing that had been compiled after the estate agent, Suzy Lamplugh, disappeared. At that time there was no missing persons helpline.

The ballet school was reopening on 23 February and,

to welcome me back, a group of the parents kindly sent flowers. Because of my back injury, however, I had arranged for a student teacher to take the classes. She was a young German girl who had just finished her training and spoke perfect English. Gerry drove me to the hall and left me there alone to prepare things and wait for the pianist while he went to pick up the young teacher from the station.

The stage was immediately above me as I rummaged about. I felt a flow of cold air and heard the outside door at the back of the stage bang. I looked up and saw the outline of a figure dressed in black. 'Trevor!' I gasped and the moment flashed past. The door opened again and my pianist, Sue, came in. She could see I was shaken but assumed it was because of the reopening of the school.

The classes went well and everyone was very kind. Returning home in the car that evening I felt very tearful and described what I had seen to Gerry. He tried to comfort me. We had only been home a short while when the doorbell rang. It was two police officers, their faces grave. They removed their hats and stepped into the hall.

'Is it bad news?' I asked.

'Yes,' they replied.

We moved into the lounge and they suggested we sat down. 'Trevor has been found dead,' one of them told us, 'on private property adjoining a local park. A young gardener discovered him in thick undergrowth this afternoon.' The discovery had been made at about the same time that I had seen the apparition on the stage. Trevor had been found dead, face downwards, on the ground. He was wearing grey trousers and a black raincoat. His blue shirt was hanging from the branch of a tree just above where he lay. Apart from his singlet, which seemed to be missing, these were the same clothes he was wearing when he disappeared. Though his body was very decomposed, they told us there was enough evidence, such as his watch, keys, papers and dental records, to prove that it was him. They seemed to be suggesting that it could be suicide.

We both sat, motionless, trying to absorb the terrible news. Gerry, who had always been so positive that Trevor would come home, went very pale and for a moment I thought he was going to faint. I asked one of the policemen to fetch Eva. For me it was confirmation of all my fears since my premonition on the first day. I had never believed that Trevor would go off without letting us know where he was staying.

'There will be a post-mortem and an inquest,' the police told us, 'and when we are satisfied with our enquiries his body will be released for burial.'

I stood up and spoke in a voice which surprised me with its firmness. 'I would like to see my son's body.'

They tried to dissuade me, warning me that it was very decomposed and would be upsetting for me, but I stood firm. After they had gone one of our neighbours said, 'Pat, if you have any doubts that it might not be Trevor, even though the police believe they have proof, you must follow your instincts. If you don't see him you might have regrets later.'

For the next two days Gerry and I talked about it endlessly. Eventually we decided that we would prefer to remember him as he was when he was alive, a tall, good-looking young man with a cheeky smile.

It was a harrowing task for two close friends, informing all the people who had been so supportive of what had happened. The next morning Trevor's close friends arrived together. We sat in the lounge, trying to gain comfort from each other. Paul, who, like Gerry, had always believed he would return, was particularly agitated. He sat for a few minutes and then jumped to his feet, his hands on his hips, eyes darting from one face to another. In a strained voice he asked, 'why, what could have happened? I don't understand.' Shaking his head he abruptly sat down, lighting a cigarette. The other lads remained subdued and Kevin, Trevor's closest friend, kept his emotions in check although he went on to suffer terrible bouts of depression for many months.

The police arranged for us to be taken, with our two close friends, Michael and Janet, to see the place where Trevor had been found. That Saturday afternoon we arrived, with two police officers, at the National Foundation for Education Research private ground in

Slough. We walked along the sloping lawns that led to dense, overgrown bushes. My whole being was racked with pain. I clung to Gerry and one of the officers as we almost had to crawl through the undergrowth to a small clearing which appeared before us like an opening in a wood. We all stood on a steep bank, surrounded by tall trees and one of the officers showed us the branch where Trevor's shirt was found hanging. It was so low I could almost touch it. We stood in the quietness with our heads bowed and the sympathetic policemen removed their hats as Michael said prayers for all of us. As I raised my head I was aware of the light from the sky flickering through the trees. Please God, I thought, help us through this anguish.

That morning Stewart and Ruth had driven to the entrance of the grounds and sat staring, in disbelief, for two hours.

The funeral was to be on Friday, 3 March. Three times the undertakers tried to arrange to collect Trevor from the hospital mortuary and take him to the Chapel of Rest, but the police did not release the body until 2 March. We had no idea what was happening. The inquest was opened on 27 February and adjourned until 10 March.

Although Trevor had not been to church recently, he did have Christian beliefs and we felt a church service would be a thanksgiving for all the love, pleasure and friendship he had given his friends and family. It would be followed by a committal at the crematorium. Gerry and I wanted to spare his friends the bleakness of the crematorium as many of them were experiencing the death of a close friend for the first time. In the end they all insisted on attending both services. I'm sure Trevor would have told me to stop making such a fuss!

I was living in a daze. We couldn't decide where his ashes should be placed. Essex Cricket Club, where Trevor had been a member, agreed to a short service and the scattering of his ashes on their Chelmsford ground but Gerry, and Trevor's friends, were in favour of burying him in holy ground, a local churchyard where he could have an inscribed tablet which they could visit.

The night before the funeral I confided to my neighbour, Sylvia, who had recently lost her husband, 'I don't know how I am going to get through tomorrow.'

'With God's support,' she replied, 'and the prayers of the many people who care for you both, it will be possible.'

We woke up to a bright, clear sky and through the morning the front lawn became covered with floral tributes. Gerry decided to wear a light grey suit because Trevor always hated seeing him in the dark, 'funeral suits' which Gerry had worn for work whenever he was visiting newly bereaved families. I wore a black coat with an orangey-pink fleck, and a light beige Kangol beret which I had worn for Trevor's christening.

As we prepared to set off, I noticed all the neighbours

quietly leaving their homes for the service, locking their doors behind them. Stepping from the car at the church I felt as if the pain was going to break my heart. There was a short pause before we could proceed and I found myself thinking about mundane things like the upstairs leaking tap and worrying about a flood. Then I felt a wave of panic that I wasn't going to be able to face the sight of Trevor's coffin in front of the altar.

The church was packed with familiar faces, some of whom had travelled a long way, and so many young people in sober clothes. For most of the service I was in a trance. Nothing that was being said, or sung, could I relate to Trevor. I was conscious of tearful people, rustling service sheets and an enormous feeling of sadness. Later the priest told us it had been a difficult service to conduct because the young people all looked so aghast, seeming to expect him to deliver some answers to the tragedy.

As Gerry and I followed the coffin out to a recording of Phil Collins' 'Against all odds' and the Pet Shop Boys singing 'You are always on my mind', I thought, this is my Trevor, these are his sounds.

The following day we returned with Jean and Harry to remove the cards from the floral tributes so that we could thank everyone personally. I walked, in drizzling rain, up and down the rows, staring at all the flowers and wreaths. Then I realised that expected flowers from my brother-in-law and sister-in-law in Spain were missing and I suddenly became hysterical. 'Someone has stolen them!' I shouted. Gerry tried to calm me, suggesting they had gone astray in transit.

Harry, who was sitting on a wall, sheltering from the rain, called out, 'let's get her out of here!'

My brother-in-law, who had flown over from Spain for the service, had been too upset to notice his missing flowers and so we never told him. The funeral directors later removed the family and close friends' tributes to their cold store. The rest of the flowers my sister and I scattered on the ground where Trevor was found. Later in the year, the proprietors planted a tree there in Trevor's memory.

My parents had not been well enough to come to the funeral and we went to visit them on Mothering Sunday. They were very supportive and tried to comfort us. Dad suggested that we employ a solicitor to represent us at the inquest. He thought we would be too upset and stressed to be able to answer questions properly and a solicitor would know how to cross-examine the pathologist in pursuit of the truth. Gerry agreed. He had been to a couple of inquests in the course of his work and knew just what an ordeal they could be for the relatives. Arriving home on the Monday, we telephoned an established local firm who agreed, after lengthy discussions, to take our case on. The solicitor asked us to accompany him to the area where Trevor was found. We explained to him that Trevor was a gentle person but the circumstances of his death appeared violent. We also asked him to consider why, if Trevor had intended to disappear, he had made so many arrangements to meet friends the following week.

On Wednesday, 7 March, Trevor's ashes were interred at the churchyard in front of Gerry, me, our priest and Michael and Janet. After the committal, the funeral directors carefully placed the still fresh flowers around the interment. Michael and Janet were so kind to us throughout that period, virtually looking after us completely for two weeks and continuing to support us over the coming months.

Arriving at the court for the inquest, I felt nauseous with anxiety and my legs were trembling. The detective sergeant who was giving evidence on behalf of the police kept his distance as if we had suddenly become the opposition. Our solicitor arrived just before we were called. We all filed into the court, along with the press.

There was a hush as the proceedings got under way and the detective sergeant told them that Trevor appeared to have been hanging by his denim shirt from the branch of the tree, then later dropped to the ground. The pathologist, when questioned by our solicitor, said, 'No exact cause of death can be given because the body was not discovered for some considerable time. However, there was a deep groove in his neck and both ankles were broken. . . .'

It was questionable as to whether the shirt could have

taken his weight as Trevor was around eleven stone and six feet tall, and the branch was so low I could easily touch it. 'Could Trevor have died in any other way?' our solicitor asked.

'Yes,' he replied, 'it's possible.'

Gerry began his statement by confirming that Trevor was a popular boy. 'He had no financial worries,' he added, 'no real problems and had everything to live for. He had many very good friends whom he met regularly and a nice girlfriend. He didn't take drugs and was only a moderate drinker. He was a very level-headed boy with a cheerful disposition and everyone who knew him could not believe he would have done a thing like this. It is so totally out of character.'

'I am not in the guessing game,' the coroner interrupted, 'we shall never know how he got there, unfortunately. I will return an open verdict, which means I don't know how he died – for sure. It is a waste of a young life. For that I can give my sympathies, but little else.'

We were numb with shock. How could Trevor's death be brushed aside so quickly? With Michael and Janet we made a bee-line for the pathologist. We wanted to know why, when they can dig up bones thousands of years old and determine approximately how old they are, he couldn't tell us what had happened to a body only two-and-a-half-months dead. He talked to us for a few moments but as far as he was concerned the matter was closed.

CHAPTER 5

Holding On

For a moment I was relieved that the terrible ordeal was over. I felt that Trevor had been vindicated from the charge of taking his own life. Our family, especially Mum and Dad, had been spared the stigma of his suicide.

The full impact of what had happened hit both Gerry and me a few days after the inquest. I often had nightmares, waking in the early hours, only to find the reality was worse than the dreams. Each morning was an agony and my days were invaded by panic attacks with profuse sweating, weakness in the leg muscles making it tiring to walk, inexplicable losses of memory and hands trembling when carrying cups and saucers.

Sometimes panic would attack in places like the supermarket. I would be standing in a queue at the check-out when suddenly I'd feel hot and bothered. I would want to call out to the check-out girl, 'if you don't hurry up I'm going to drop this shopping right here and leave the shop.' On one occasion I did exactly that, feeling I would explode if I didn't get outside. Then there were the absent-minded days when I would park the car and stroll up the High Street, my mind on other things. Suddenly, thinking that I hadn't put any money in the meter, I would run back to the car park, knocking into people on the way, only to discover that I had paid after all. I was exhausted and my legs felt like jelly.

My moods were unpredictable, swinging from angry shouting to uncontrollable sobbing. All I wanted to know was – why? I talked to everyone who would listen, desperately searching for some sort of answer. I realised that only a mother who has suffered a similar loss can understand how impossible it is to let go of a child. Their spirit is part of you until the end of your life.

I kept turning over the facts in my mind. Had the knock on his head at work been instrumental in his disappearance? Should the pathologist have reconsidered the possible effects of that blow? Trevor had gone out with money in his pockets that morning, but none was found on him; had he been abducted and dragged into the undergrowth? He was a very conscientious, responsible young man, I couldn't believe he would willingly have let down all the people he had made arrangements with for the following week.

Then I would think about the role of the police. It

was evident, with hindsight, that Gerry and I had allowed ourselves to be swept along by the circumstances. Just after Trevor disappeared the police remarked that if he was still in the area they would find him, and that with all the local publicity no landlady would harbour him. So why did they not use sniffer dogs in the area where his body was found? Though a private ground it was accessible to members of the public who were attending educational courses at the Foundation. Also, bearing in mind that it is only a few yards from the High Street where Gerry had said goodbye to Trevor and only a mile from our home, if Trevor had been found earlier he might still have been alive, or information as to how he died might not have been lost, and we would all have been spared the distressing months of searching.

I went over and over the time leading up to his disappearance, trying to see if there had been any signs that he had a problem which would have caused him to take his own life. There was the time, while working for British Rail at the beginning of 1988 that the books hadn't balanced after a working shift; that had worried him. Also, working late at night, staff were sometimes subjected to threatening behaviour from the public. At the time Trevor had seemed edgy and disturbed. I persuaded him to see a doctor who gave him an absentee note, but Gerry was furious with me. 'You're no help, suggesting that,' he said, 'it's you who needs your head looking at!'

After that, Trevor got the job at the RAC, organising car rallies, and went on a happy summer holiday to Majorca with his friends. The job turned out to be rather tedious and technical and not the stepping stone he had hoped for to other sporting interests. Although it didn't appear to make him unhappy, he wasn't prepared to 'mark time'.

Then there was his relationship with Beth. She was a sweet person but he hadn't felt she was the right one for him. Trevor was always looking for someone to replace his first love, Kate, whom he met when 17 years old while staying with my parents. She was from the north and it turned out she had other boyfriends at home. He seemed to brood about her for several years afterwards, and would have liked to have found someone else like her. His gang of close friends were all acquiring steady girlfriends and Trevor might have worried that he would soon lose their companionship. With Gerry retiring we had been thinking of moving to the south coast to be near my parents. He might have found the coming changes unsettling. Gerry was under a lot of stress towards the end of his career and I did lean on Trevor for advice and guidance. He was always very supportive and reassuring.

'Dad comes from good stock,' he would remind me, 'he has two brothers who survived prisoner of war camps. Don't worry, Mum, he'll make it to retirement.'

I wanted Trevor to persuade his father to take it easier

at work. He did talk to him, but told me that I was also overdoing things, worrying about pupils whose parents were pushing them into taking dancing exams too early. 'You must put your foot down,' he said, 'say "no" if they are not up to it, don't give them all these free lessons.'

Trevor always enjoyed a cigarette and had no desire to kick the habit but, about two weeks before his disappearance, smoking started to make him feel sick. The doctor suggested he try giving up and prescribed nicotine gum. I rang Smokers Anonymous after his death and they explained that he could have been experiencing some inner turmoil, which would have explained the smoking sickness.

So, Trevor did have a few problems, it was true, but none that I could believe would bring him to that terrible end. I was aware that he had two sides to his personality. On the one hand he was an extrovert, a skilful conversationalist, good at putting on an act, Trevor would always see the funny side of everything. But in later years he had become more serious and was often deep in thought. His collection of records and tapes suggested a more melancholy side to his nature.

A few months after the inquest I moved into a transitional period, a sort of limbo in which my life seemed empty, my senses dulled. I could work up no interest in anything in the outside world. I was worn out in body and spirit with virtually no powers of concentration left.

The smallest task would exhaust me. I kept thinking, what is the point of living?

Time just kept ticking away and eventually, on my better days, I would be able to allow precious thoughts of the happy times enjoyed with Trevor, to seep into my mind without causing me to burst into tears. Sometimes I would even smile or half laugh, but always the piercing pain would return with the realisation that I would never see my son again.

Gerry avoided talking about Trevor, finding it distressed him too much. If we received post addressed to Trevor he would deal with the matter quickly and the conversation would abruptly be brought to an end. Soon we all learnt never to mention Trevor's name in Gerry's presence. The diaries he had written during the period Trevor was missing were relegated to the top of the wardrobe and not referred to again. Sometimes my emotions felt like a pressure cooker inside me as the events continued to churn in my mind.

After the inquest a detective sergeant called round with a few of Trevor's possessions. 'We say in the police force,' he told us, 'the first twenty five years of your life are the best, then it's downhill. Though it can only be a small comfort, you did have Trevor for twenty two years.' The remark seemed rather insensitive at the time but gradually I started to understand what he meant. Those twenty two years are the most precious thing I have.

A friend of mine, Kate, got together with a group of pupils' mothers from the ballet school at Datchet. 'We need to give Pat something to come back to,' she suggested. With the support of the young student teacher and Sue, the pianist, the parents took over the numerous tasks of running the school. I gradually started popping in and out to see them as I grew stronger through the summer term. Classes also recommenced at St Francis, Langley, with the same student teacher and David, my Langley pianist, who had kindly played for Trevor's funeral.

During the spring, two former clients of Gerry's paid for a four day holiday to Paris. It was a retirement present to say thank you for his conscientious handling of their affairs over the years. Gerry and I walked together in the warm sunshine, only vaguely aware of the beauty of the city all around us. Ambling along one winding path I caught sight of a group of young people laughing and fooling around on the lush grass of the park. Captivated by their exuberance, I imagined it was Trevor and his friends. I found that by entering a make-believe world I could momentarily relieve my heartache.

Family and friends were always trying to impress upon us how important we were to them and how much they loved us, trying hard to fill our emptiness. Our doctor arranged counselling for us at the local hospital. Sitting in the waiting room, watching other patients who either had vacant looks in their eyes or were fidgeting and distressed, I wondered if I was going mad. The sessions seemed to dig right into my heart and always reduced me to tears. We would be counselled separately for the first half of each session, then they would bring us together for the second half. At one session we were asked to write down five different reasons why we felt disappointed in each other. The intention was to bring to the surface any subconscious resentments we harboured about the way Trevor had been brought up. Then we had to list five reasons why we were each disappointed in Trevor. Gerry and I had no real secrets from one another. He knew that for many years I had thought he worked too hard and didn't spend enough time with our son. A few members of the family, including my mother, felt that I was equally guilty of that. We had both been disappointed when Trevor had decided not to go to university. It was trivial stuff but it hurt to bring it to the surface again. After those sessions I felt my soul had been exposed. They were exhausting experiences. At the time it all seemed of little help but perhaps it did put some issues into perspective.

My health was still very poor and, since we had a small private insurance policy from his work, Gerry thought it was time for me to see a consultant. I had lost so much weight it was painful even to sit on a chair, I always needed a cushion. In the bath I had to sit on a rubber sponge. The consultant was concerned about this, since I did not have enough flesh covering my vital organs. He thought he could improve my back problem with physiotherapy. 'It's muscle scarring,' he told me, 'from the original injury. The stress you are suffering is still delaying the recovery.'

At the first session of physiotherapy I could hardly raise my leg. Considering how fit I had once been the deterioration was unbelievable. I made an enormous effort to go swimming, but once in the pool I would first suffer agonizing cramp, then there was the ordeal of getting dried and dressed. But, as the weeks passed, my physical condition gradually improved.

1989 was a very warm summer and the sun would often beat down on my head as I walked along the winding Langley Road to St Mary's Churchyard, Trevor's resting place. I found it hard to believe, as I bent to arrange flowers, that it was Trevor's gravestone.

One hot afternoon, out shopping with Gerry in Slough High Street, there was a bomb scare in a large store and the police were everywhere. Many of the officers recognised us and removed their hats in acknowledgement. I felt sad that we had become so well-known by the Slough and Langley constabulary because of the loss of Trevor.

My Aunt Joan and her ex-business partner, who was also called Joan, invited my parents, Gerry and me to their home in Florida for Christmas. Although we were made to feel very welcome and the sunshine did us good, when we returned to England, we found our house had been broken into. Then, a few weeks later, two dear friends died. It seemed as if the misery was never going to cease.

As time went by I turned my attentions to work, moving slowly away from teaching ballet towards teaching gentle, therapeutic yoga, although in 1991 I did complete the course for the Royal Academy of Dancing's new children's syllabus. I felt that if I had no goals I would simply fall apart. I wanted passionately to do something worthwhile with my life. I threw myself into so many different activities that often the effort made me ill. Two years after Trevor's death my mother suffered a stroke. Whilst helping with her rehabilitation I became interested in teaching remedial work and completed a St John's Ambulance First Aid course.

To keep depression at bay it is essential to be physically well. I have found yoga to be a powerful weapon in the fight against anxiety. The asanas or postures help to stretch and strengthen various parts of the body and breathing correctly aids physical and mental relaxation.

Gerry was very supportive of all my activities but found little to motivate himself, despite keeping up his hobbies of tennis, art and beginners' yoga. In the summer of 1991 he was diagnosed as having mild diabetes. That, combined with periods of depression, caused tiredness and he needed to take more rest. After retiring he had intended going back two days a week to his old company, but was too mentally and physically drained. I think if he had pushed himself to do that it might have helped him back to some normality. As it was, on 15 January 1993, Gerry came home from the library, opened the lounge door and said to me, 'Hello, I can see you're busy.' He then closed the door, went upstairs, propped himself up on the bed, crossed his legs, folded his arms and died of a heart attack. I found him five or ten minutes later.

Disaster had struck again in less than four years and I thought the unbelievable shock would kill me.

CHAPTER 6

Going on Without Gerry

I tried to resuscitate Gerry, but, when there was no response, ran for Eva. When she returned, she called for an ambulance and I continued my efforts to bring him back. While waiting for help to arrive we both tried to revive him. The ambulance men also tried, with all their sophisticated equipment.

'I'm sorry,' one of the men said after a few minutes, 'your husband has gone.'

He's now out of all that dreadful misery, I thought, and I just wish I could have gone with him.

Later, the paramedics reassured me that I had followed the correct procedure by clearing his airways, as this enabled them to quickly start their resuscitation attempts. Because it was a sudden death, a doctor and the police had to be advised. Eva telephoned friends and neighbours who were soon on the spot. The doctor was delayed and then had difficulty finding the road. Several people made tea. The vicar was away at the time and came home to find his answering machine jammed with messages about the passing of Gerry Holman.

Everyone wanted me to stay the night in another house but I was determined not to, believing that if I didn't do it the first time I would never be able to stay in the house alone. Poor Eva spent most of the night peering through her curtains across the road to check I was okay. In fact, I knocked myself out with a sleeping pill and slept heavily. Although there had been so much sadness in the house, there was no bad atmosphere. I have never felt that I would have to move because of unpleasant memories. In many ways I feel that both Trevor and Gerry are still there with me.

I had now lost two of the people I most loved. How, when engulfed in such misery, could I hold on to my Christian beliefs? On top of that worry was the panic of how to cope with life on my own. Gerry, having had legal training, had always seen to all the household administration, and the thought of managing alone was frightening. I had lost my companion, supporter, DIY man and legal adviser all at once.

Friends and neighbours came to my rescue again, taking over all the arrangements for the funeral. While we waited for the post-mortem, two friends, Terry and Carole, patiently accompanied me on the various tasks that have to be dealt with when somebody dies, such as collecting the death certificate. There is so much red tape and it is hard to focus and concentrate when you are full of grief. Eva would knock on my door each day to check I was alright and that I was doing my exercises and breathing practice, both of which she was sure were going to be integral to my recovery.

St Francis' Church was packed with people and flowers for Gerry's thanksgiving service, many people having to stand. Both the priest, John, and our friend Michael included Trevor in their addresses. The service at the church was followed by the committal at the crematorium. One of Gerry's brothers and my great friend Doris, from Essex, missed the church service due to roadworks on the M25, but came to the crematorium. Doris flung her arms around me.

'You're looking great girl,' she said, 'come on, let's give him a good send off.'

As John was taking the service the door to the crematorium squeaked open slowly. John paused for a moment and the congregation followed his gaze to where Kevin was standing with his recently broken leg in plaster. He had not been able to walk as fast as everyone else and had been left behind coming from a friend's car. John, understandingly, waited before continuing whilst he got seated.

I had known Doris since I was ten years old. My parents decided, when the war in Europe ended in 1945, to move from Newport in Shropshire to be nearer London. We settled in Leigh-on-Sea in Essex and I found it hard to adjust, being teased about my broad North Country accent. Doris was one of my first southern friends and we had stayed in touch for nearly fifty years.

The mourners filled three houses, including mine, after the service. Gerry, who was quiet and unassuming, would have been staggered that so many people turned up to say farewell. Doris, trying to be sociable with my Slough friends, told them what good fun we had in our youth. Because of my love of dance, she said, she had never envisaged me getting married.

After Trevor's funeral no one had eaten or talked much, but after Gerry's there was hardly a thing left. In a way everyone felt Gerry had died from a broken heart and had now been released from his distress.

Terry kindly accompanied me to the Probate Court. Although Gerry had all our financial affairs in order, an insurance policy that had been paid out on Trevor's death was still left in Gerry's name. He had found it too painful to deal with. Parents do not want to inherit from their children.

Two months after my husband's death I returned to the sports centre to teach yoga and spent the summer considering what to do about the ballet school. When discussing it with my sister, Jean, she warned me of the dangers of giving up dancing, which had meant so much to me all my life, at the same time as losing so much else.

I started learning to dance after recovering from pneumonia at six years old. I nearly died, as there were no antibiotics in those days, and was left very susceptible to chesty colds. In desperation my mother took me to see a German specialist who suggested sending me to dancing classes to develop my chest muscles and help with my breathing. I became very enthusiastic and ended up at professional dancing schools as a teenager, going on to become a full-time student of dance and drama, knowing from a very early age that, although not especially gifted, I wanted to specialise in teaching ballet. It was during my student days that I met Gerry, at a Saturday night hop. He was five years older than me and had just completed National Service. While establishing myself as a teacher, I worked as an assistant stage manager in repertory and took on some professional dance engagements as well as television and modelling work. In my twenties I taught underprivileged children at the Mary Ward Settlement at Tavistock Place in King's Cross for three years, which had a profound influence on my teaching methods.

Gerry had no experience of theatrical life but was very supportive of my career, giving me ideas for props and costumes and helping backstage at the numerous dance school displays. He organised the proceeds from these events for charities and willingly helped pupils with their form filling for exams.

A year after our marriage we bought an old house and together converted it into a dance studio with living accommodation. It was an enormous task, with little

cash, which we both threw ourselves into. Even though
Gerry was starting his career with the Trust Company at
the same time, he was incredibly supportive of me. I
went on teaching throughout our marriage and various
moves around the country. Dancing had been my life
but after the loss of the two loved ones most precious to
me, it became insignificant. Six months on my own and
away from dancing, I thought there would be too much
worry if I reopened the school. Teaching yoga at the
sports centre and running the home and car absorbed all
my energies. A teacher I had known for a few years
agreed to take over the ballet school. There was nothing
in exchange: I gave away my dancing school. As I said
goodbye to many of my pupils and their parents, I
thought sadly, life has worn me out, my dancing days
have gone forever. After what had happened the value of
what I had built up did not seem to matter any more.

In those months I had a strange surge of nervous
energy. I can remember seeing, from the kitchen window, a bush that needed attention. I rushed out into the
garden with the shears and energetically cut it into
shape. Then, in the heat of the moment, I creosoted the
garden shed, dropping much of it onto the lawn. When
the washing line became entangled I attacked it with a
pair of scissors in my desperation.

It was also a time when a number of household gadgets
packed up on me and had to be replaced, even the television went up in smoke. There was all the hassle of trying

to learn to work the replacement items. I had to sell my car as I was going to use Gerry's. My parents placed a card in a shop window near them and fortunately a couple agreed to buy it and kindly drove me back from West Sussex to Slough. Gestures like that make a big difference in life. Dennis and his wife Jean, two very kind neighbours, came to my rescue many times: cutting grass, adjusting a shower that only spouted boiling hot water, repairing leaking taps and providing nourishing meals and home-made cakes. They were like guardian angels. My confidence gradually grew with each little achievement, whether it was mastering the time clock on the gas boiler or working the video, conquering the electric mower or planting out the flower beds, changing light bulbs, touching up paintwork or even washing and hanging curtains. As I struggled to acquire new skills I realised how unobservant I had been during my life. My knowledge of car maintenance has slightly improved although Dennis does check the car regularly. I had to overcome my fears of driving in unfamiliar places and on the motorways to my parents' home.

Losing your partner and no longer being part of a couple changes your friendships. I found it excluded me from some social functions although several of my friends showed great consideration on awkward occasions. Some people suddenly withdrew their support, perhaps thinking I might become a burden, whereas others were untiring in their efforts to help. My friends, in the dark early days of bereavement, were my life-line.

I tried hard to be cheerful in company and remember that other people have their own problems. It was important to cultivate a wide cross-section of helpful and social friends so that I didn't lean too much on any one person, but there remain a few special friends who, even if I don't see them very often, are always there with help and support. Learning to help myself has been essential. I think dance training gave me a strength which has contributed to my survival.

Sometimes, when invited somewhere, I have been hesitant to accept, making excuses of feeling tired when really I am just wanting to withdraw from life. I have to nag myself out loud, forcing myself to get out of the house before I lose all my friends. Having reluctantly accepted whatever the invitation is, I always return home feeling better, more alive and thankful that other people have not given up on me.

During the following autumn, Gerry's brother, Tony, and his wife, Rita, invited me to their home in Spain for a holiday. Whilst walking on the beach I knew on my return home I wanted to face up to everything that had happened by writing it down in book form to help others who find themselves in similar situations. A death like Trevor's leaves so many unanswered questions. What happened to Gerry and me could happen to anyone, any family can be struck by an unexpected and mysterious death. There are certain things which I have come to believe very strongly after my experiences: one is that however expert the police become with the use of new technology, they must not lose sight of the importance of early searching. It would greatly assist vulnerable and distressed relatives if there could be a police officer on-hand who, as in rape cases, specialises in the handling of relatives of missing people.

The coroner's open verdict means we will never know the true circumstances of Trevor's death; never have anyone or anything to blame, nothing at which to direct our anger and hurt. I continue to search in my mind for fresh clues but only find guilt at not knowing, not seeing if there were any danger signals that could have alerted us to what was going to happen.

Counselling is helpful after a tragedy, assisting people to come to terms with their uncertainties and the changes that have taken place in their lives. I felt so guilty and angry after both the deaths of my loved ones that I often believed my powers of reasoning had deserted me. Life, with all its worries and fears, appeared so black, so pointless. Confiding in friends often helped to put things back into perspective.

Having been unable to resuscitate Gerry I began to question the worth of the St John's Ambulance Public First Aid course I had taken, but, whilst staying with my parents the following Christmas my father's heart stopped beating. It was New Year's Eve and I was in the kitchen preparing lunch when my mother called me from the lounge. Dad, then 86 years old, was slumped in a chair with no pulse. He looked very pale. I immediately checked his airways to make sure there was no obstruction and then commenced resuscitation. Within a few moments his heart started beating again. After a short spell in hospital he was sent home with a prescription for a low dose of aspirin to be taken daily to thin his blood.

Afterwards, on my way back to Slough, I started reflecting on Trevor and Gerry's deaths. It seemed unfair that I had not been given any second chance to try to help them. But perhaps they didn't want help. Neither had said they felt depressed or unwell. I love them both dearly and would have done anything to have saved them. I'm just glad I didn't have a crystal ball to see what was coming.

Trevor was my only child, it is hard to accept the reality that he has gone from my life, and for a long time his death made me apathetic about everything else. If the tiles had fallen off the roof of the house I wouldn't have cared less. When I was flying down to Spain the plane had to make an emergency landing because a passenger had suffered a heart attack. I felt almost immune to the chaos that was going on around me, the incident seemed to make no impact on me. It became hard to see the purpose in anything. When I heard people worrying about getting their planting done, or about their children's examination grades, marriages or mis-demeanours, I felt like shaking them and shouting, 'nobody's died!' Life is the only important thing and the fragile line between it and death can break at any moment. If only Trevor was alive I wouldn't have cared if he had robbed the Bank of England.

A few weeks after my dear son's death one of my contemporaries told me she was expecting her first grandchild. I was speechless because for me there would never be any grandchildren, my future had been swept away with Trevor. When he was alive I would have been horrified at the thought of him, a young man, being burdened with a baby. Loss changes so many concepts.

I love to talk about Trevor and fortunately Kevin and Paul still visit me regularly. We chat about the old days and the antics they got up to. They tell me it was the happiest time of their lives when they were with Trevor. In those days they were frequent visitors to our home, cheerfully suffering my threats of dire trouble if the house was left like a tip. These days I find myself hoovering before they visit. They have grown into fine young men with properties of their own. Subconsciously I don't want them to grow old, wishing they could be locked in time with Trevor and finding myself resenting any changes that Trevor can't be here to witness. It is hard to listen to music on the radio as there are often songs being played from the 1980s that remind me so much of him. Sometimes he would have the radio, his music centre and the television all going at once in different rooms as he drifted around the house, singing and humming, sometimes even going out, leaving all the music still blaring.

Lately, whilst strolling along the promenade on holiday, groups of high spirited young men have come towards me and briefly I have thought they were Trevor and his friends. It has made me feel both happy and sad, wanting to urge them to enjoy every minute of their lives. Remembering Trevor's dry sense of humour sometimes makes me laugh out loud when sitting alone, thinking how quick he was at turning a slightly serious situation into something light-hearted, cleverly releasing tensions.

I have little interest in cooking now. I told a counsellor that I could no longer make Trevor's favourite chocolate cake. 'Don't push yourself too hard,' the counsellor advised, 'buy a cake.' My memory recall has been poor ever since his death. It is nature's way of blotting out pain, but unfortunately other information has also been erased like travel routes and places I visited. All these kinds of things have made me feel a lesser person.

During the first year I did feel Trevor's presence quite often. Opening the broom cupboard a scent of his cigarette smoke would pull me up in my tracks. But if I tried to recapture the moment it just disappeared like an elusive dream. Gerry said he never had these experiences, although Jean and Harry did. Now I feel his spirit has moved on, though he is still keeping an eye on me from afar. When life is difficult and I am feeling down, I can almost hear him saying, 'Come on Mum, don't give up.' Now it is the quietness of the house that makes me feel sad. I miss the arguments, the snippets of gossip and the sounds of youth. At first, after he died, I desperately wanted to believe in an afterlife, unable to bear the thought of never seeing him again. There have been many moments since Gerry's death when problems seemed overwhelming and in my desolation I have turned to God for guidance. My prayers often seem to be answered indirectly. A friend would unexpectedly telephone or call at the house and the conversation would drift towards whatever was worrying me and a solution would nearly always emerge. Having lost everything that was most precious to me in this life I have come to realise that the only way forward is to follow my Christian beliefs. All through the eighties I think I was looking for something more than the cluttered materialistic world that I was part of.

These days I tend to tire easily. Lying out on the settee one very hot summer's day, I remembered the premonition I had on the day Trevor disappeared and the turret-like building which had sprung into my mind. I had a sudden thought. Jumping up and going out to the car I drove myself to the place where he was found. My heart was racing as I walked through the grounds and stared up at the building. To my amazement, looming towards the sky, was this turret-edged structure. Why had I never thought to look up there before?

In 1994 my sister's youngest daughter produced a lovely baby girl, making my parents into great grandparents the same year as they celebrated their sixtieth wedding anniversary. Sadly, my longest-standing friend, Doris, died that year from cancer while still in her fifties. It was very distressing returning to Essex for the funeral, but I was also very upset at the christening, seeing such a large gathering of young people, many with their offspring and thinking how my life would have been enriched if I'd had grandchildren.

The anger and bitterness that I felt at the premature deaths of Trevor and Gerry have passed now. Gerry's ashes are buried next to Trevor's. Their resting place was once a rose garden. In the summer many butterflies appear and there is always a sweet smell in the air from the blossoming trees and flowers. I like to think they are now both at rest in God's care. Letting them both go to Him has been my most difficult task of all.

Trevor

Trevor's close friends' sentiments:

> Trev – we miss your sense of humour
> That cheeky smile
> The natural ease that friends always
> Felt when in your company
> But most of all we think of loyalty
> That you gave to us – your mates.

CHAPTER 7

What to do if it Happens to You

To have a loved one go missing can be as agonizing as the finality of death. Living with the unknown and the constant strain of searching is both mentally and physically debilitating.

Of the countless people reported missing each year, many either return home of their own volition or are safely found, but the relatives still need the same levels of support through the searching stages.

Society is becoming more aware of the need to provide help and support for the families of missing people. The confidential Missing Person's Helpline and the local police forces' closer links with Scotland Yard's computer register of missing people are both important steps forward. They are the beginning of a lifeline, not only for the distressed families but possibly also for the missing person who, for whatever reason, feels the need to withdraw from the life they know.

When a person goes missing there are many things you can do:

1. STAY CALM.
2. Contact their friends, both new and old, their relations both close and distant, their places of work, clubs and hospitals.
3. Check their passports are still at home.
4. Contact their bank, building society, credit card company or post office to see if any money has been withdrawn.
5. Inform the local police. They will note the information and, once satisfied the person is missing, will compile a comprehensive report. The information is then circulated by computer to stations all round the country – it is known as the National Identification Bureau. Subsequently the facts are passed to the National Independent Register, where the missing person's details are registered under the section Information Related. The various branches do liaise with one another.
6. Phone the charity, National Missing Persons Helpline, Freephone 0500 700-700 (24 hour service), or write to them at Roebuck House, 284–286 Upper Richmond Road West, East Sheen, London SW14 7JE. Telephone 0181 392-2000, during office hours.
7. Get in touch with local press and radio in your area and any area where the missing person had previous associations.

8. Ask the organisers of public address systems at sports venues such as football grounds. They are always willing to oblige.

9. Obtain a copy of the BBC Family Directory from a good bookshop or direct from Customer Service, Health Education Authority, PO Box 269, Abingdon, Oxfordshire OX14 4YN. Telephone 01235 465565/6. This excellent booklet contains the functions and addresses of over 160 organisations providing help and information to families.

There are organisations to help those who have been suddenly bereaved:

1. The Compassionate Friends, 53 North Street, Bristol BS3 1EN. Helpline: 0117 953 9639. This is a nation-wide and international self-help organisation of parents whose children of any age have died through accident, illness, murder or suicide.

2. Cruse (bereavement care), Cruse House, 126 Sheen Road, Richmond, Surrey TW9 1UR. Helpline: 0181 332 7227 (9.30 a.m.–5 p.m. Mon–Fri). Cruse offers free help to all bereaved people through many local branches by providing both individual and group counselling, opportunities for social contact and practical advice.

The Inquest – Coroner's Court:

1. An inquest explains how death occurred – not why.

2. It is an enquiry not a trial.
3. The coroner has the power to decide the verdict.
4. Relatives do not have the right to know the evidence police have obtained before a case.
5. It is sometimes better to be legally represented. Relatives are often too upset and nervous to make clear statements or to reply to questions in a precise and clear manner.
6. An open verdict does not reveal how someone died. Controversial deaths must be properly investigated and the introduction of new laws is being considered.

Probate Court

It is advisable to have legal representation and this means that you do not have to attend the court yourself. If you are not legally represented then ensure you are accompanied by a good and supportive friend.